Portsmouth Black Heritage Trail

A Self-Guided Walking Tour of Portsmouth, New Hampshire

ISBN: 978-1-938394-33-1

Library of Congress Control Number 2018958692

Published by

Black Heritage Trail of New Hampshire
222 Court Street
Portsmouth NH 03801

blackheritagetrailnh.org

Designed and produced by
Grace Peirce
Great Life Press
Rye, NH 03870

www.greatlifepress.com

Contributing editors: Anne Arnold, JerriAnne Boggis, Valerie Cunningham, Angela Matthews, Grace Peirce, Cathy Wolff

Photos courtesy of: John Benford Photography, JerriAnne Boggis, Valerie Cunningham, Rose Downes, Angela Matthews, David J. Murray, Grace Peirce, Joanna Raptis, Sara Schoman, Portsmouth Athenaeum, Atlantic Media, and Black Heritage Trail of New Hampshire

The Black Heritage Trail of New Hampshire

works to visibly honor and share a truer more inclusive history through exhibits, programs, and tours that can change the way our country understands human dignity when it is free of historical stereotypes.

Vision

To celebrate a people's history of resilience, versatility, and courage.

Mission

To promote awareness and appreciation of African-American history in New Hampshire.

Purpose

To promote awareness and appreciation of African-American history in New Hampshire through education and public programs, including creating appropriate memorials at significant locations within the state.

Contents

Welcome Friends

We tell New Hampshire's forgotten stories

From the docks of Portsmouth, where merchants engaged in the trans-Atlantic slave trade unloaded their cargo, to the northern border with Canada, where many escaping captives found their first moment of freedom, the Granite State holds a multitude of stories that mark the milestones of its complex history.

For more than 300 years, the lives of African people and their descendants have been a part of New Hampshire's history. African-American history has long been hidden in the shadows even though Black lives have been intermixing with White lives in highly personal ways.

The Black Heritage Trail of New Hampshire works to open hearts and minds to a deeper understanding of who we are as a collective and to recognize that we share a uniquely American heritage.

Building on our success with the Portsmouth Black Heritage Trail that started more than two decades ago, the new Black Heritage Trail of New Hampshire will connect the stories of New Hampshire's African heritage by documenting and making visible historic sites that testify to this rich history.

Guided tours and public programs, along with educational materials and teacher workshops, will continue to be developed by the Black Heritage Trail to promote awareness of African-American culture and to honor all the people of African descent whose names may not have been included in previous town histories.

As we celebrate a people's history of resilience, versatility and courage, we invite everyone to explore for themselves what our shared history means and bring that understanding into the present.

JerriAnne Boggis
Executive Director
Black Heritage Trail of New Hampshire

Valerie Cunningham
Founding Member
Portsmouth Black Heritage Trail

Our African Heritage

Portsmouth, New Hampshire has been home to Africans and African-Americans for more than 350 years. Upon examination of their stories, we find that against the odds of early enslavement and subsequent marginalization, Africans and their descendants built communities and families, founded institutions, and served their town, state, and nation in many capacities.

New Hampshire has an African heritage that dates back almost to the arrival of Europeans. Much of that history centers on the state's only port at Portsmouth. As many as 700 Blacks were here by the Revolution; many were caught up in an active Northern slave market while others were part of a little-known free society.

The first known Black person in Portsmouth came from the west coast of Africa in 1645. He was captured one Sunday when slave merchants attacked his village in Guinea, killing about a hundred persons and wounding others. Upon arrival in Boston, the slave was bought by a Mr. Williams "of Piscataqua." When the General Court of the colony learned of the raid and kidnapping, it ordered the captives to be returned to their African home. Slavery was not the issue of concern, for human bondage was legal in the region. The court was "indignant" that raiders had violated the Sabbath with the "haynos and crying sin of man stealing."

> New Hampshire has an African heritage that dates back almost to the arrival of Europeans.

The size of the Black population in seventeenth-century New Hampshire was small and, therefore, easily overlooked. However, surveys of wills and inventories show that slaves were included in the estates of several prominent early Portsmouth families. Additional evidence that "mulattoes, Negroes and slaves" were present can be found in laws which were adopted around the turn of the century. They were similar to the restrictive laws enacted in other colonies which controlled activities of both servants and masters. Laws prohibited servants from roaming through town without their master's permission, being "abroad in the night time after nine o'clock," and drinking in public taverns.

Downtown Portsmouth

Today's downtown includes sites of the earliest urban settlement, the waterfront, homes of the early merchants, and, consequently, the earliest enslavements. Enslavement of Africans was part of Portsmouth life by 1645, although the first records of Portsmouth merchants participating in the slave trade were in the 1680s, with captives mostly male children and adolescents sold directly from ship or dockside near the area where Prescott Park is now. A 1775 census reported 656 enslaved Africans in New Hampshire, mostly in Portsmouth and adjacent towns. Since colonial times, Portsmouth's population has remained 2 to 4 percent Black.

Downtown Portsmouth Map Key

1 †Black Heritage Trail of New Hampshire office, 222 Court St.

2 Governor John Langdon House, 143 Pleasant St.

3 William Pitt Tavern, 416 Court St., Strawbery Banke Museum

4 *†Docks & view of Portsmouth Naval Shipyard, Prescott Park

5 Sherburne House, Strawbery Banke campus

6 South Meeting House, 280 Marcy St.

7 *NH Gazette, corner of Howard & Washington Streets [private]

8 †Cooper House & Beauty Shop, 171 Washington St. [private]

9 Stoodley's Tavern, 14 Hancock St., Strawbery Banke Museum

10 Penhallow House, 93 Washington St., Strawbery Banke Museum

11 †Warner House, 150 Daniel St.

12 Saint John's Church, 100 Chapel St.

13 Waterfront, Ceres Street

14 Moffatt-Ladd House, 154 Market St.

15 *Black Whipple House, 127 High St. [private]

16 Meeting Rooms, 14-16 Market Square, corner of Daniel & Pleasant Streets

17 *†Town Pump and Stocks, next to North Church

18 North Church, Market Square

19 *†Pomp & Candace Spring House & Bakery, Church Street

20 *The Music Hall (The Temple), Chestnut Street at Congress Street

21 †John Paul Jones House, 43 Middle St.

22 Rockingham House, 401 State St. [private]

23 African Burying Ground, Chestnut Street, between Court & State Streets

24 South Church, 292 State St.

* The original structure no longer exists

† No descriptive plaque

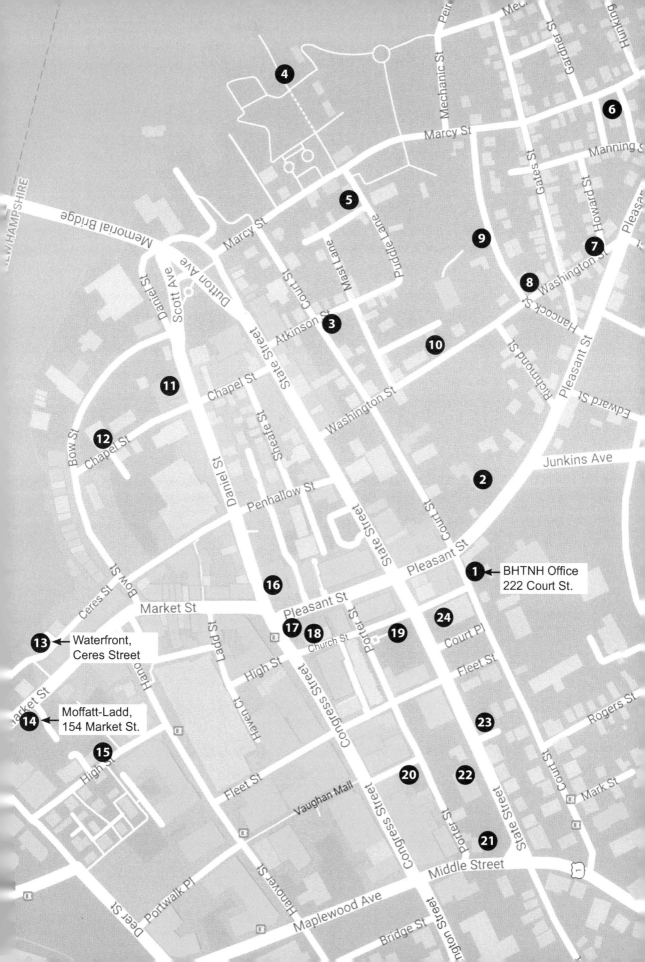

1 ← BHTNH Office
222 Court St.

13 ← Waterfront,
Ceres Street

14 ← Moffatt-Ladd,
154 Market St.

Black Heritage Trail of New Hampshire Office, 222 Court St.

Home to the Black Heritage Trail of New Hampshire (BHTNH), this house was built c. 1740. It was the parsonage of Reverend Arthur Browne, the first minister of the Episcopal Church in Portsmouth, formerly the Queen's Chapel (site 12). Browne bequeathed at least two of his enslaved persons, Pompey and Jesse, to his wife and nephew when he died in 1773.

The Black Heritage Trail of New Hampshire purchased the 222 Court St. property in 2018 for its new home. "We're creating a new space where we can tell a more inclusive state history story," Executive Director JerriAnne Boggis said.

The new headquarters will be an anchor for statewide educational tours and the building will also house a research and visitors center.

Board President Robert Thompson and Executive Director JerriAnne Boggis iin front of the historic building to be converted from law offices to the new home of the Black Heritage Trail of New Hampshire.

† No descriptive plaque

Governor John Langdon House, 143 Pleasant St.

Cyrus Bruce, formerly enslaved, was working for John Langdon as a paid servant by 1783 when Langdon was building this mansion on Pleasant Street. He served as Langdon's valet and butler, wearing an impressive costume of dark broadcloth coat, ruffles, silk stockings, silver-buckled shoes, and a gold chain with seals. He received part of his pay in cash, part in goods, and, by 1797, part in housing. He and his wife, the former Flora Stoodley (sites 9 & 18), lived behind the mansion in one of two houses Governor Langdon owned on Washington Street. Cyrus was no doubt present when George Washington dined at the mansion in November 1789 and also may have been of assistance to Ona Judge (sites 31 & 35), who escaped Washington's household in 1796 and fled to Portsmouth.

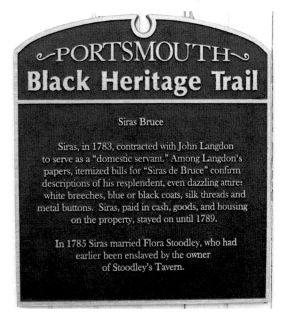

~PORTSMOUTH~
Black Heritage Trail

Siras Bruce

Siras, in 1783, contracted with John Langdon to serve as a "domestic servant." Among Langdon's papers, itemized bills for "Siras de Bruce" confirm descriptions of his resplendent, even dazzling attire: white breeches, blue or black coats, silk threads and metal buttons. Siras, paid in cash, goods, and housing on the property, stayed on until 1789.

In 1785 Siras married Flora Stoodley, who had earlier been enslaved by the owner of Stoodley's Tavern.

William Pitt Tavern, 416 Court St., at Strawbery Banke Museum

This three-story tavern, built in 1766, is remembered as the scene of Revolutionary turmoil and visits of famous patriots. Its owner, John Stavers, was once charged with beating someone else's Black servant. He also auctioned people imported from the West Indies; advertised for his runaway sixteen-year-old slave, Fortune; and charged a fee to view a nine-year-old albino African boy. In 1777, Mark Noble, suspicious of Stavers' patriotism (the tavern was suspected of hosting Tory meetings), began chopping down the tavern sign. Stavers sent his slave James to stop him. James knocked Noble unconscious and then, according to legend, hid in a cistern in the basement, afraid of retribution. Stavers was arrested and tried for suspected disloyalty, but James was neither arrested nor

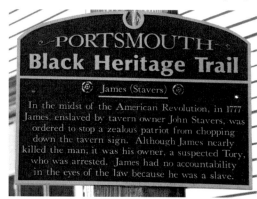

charged with assault. An enslaved person's status, identity, and actions were the responsibility of his owner or another White who directed him. For example, when two neighboring women forced James to steal food from the tavern, they—not James—were charged with theft.

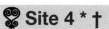

Docks & View of the Portsmouth Naval Shipyard, Prescott Park

The first records of Portsmouth merchants participating in the slave trade were in the 1680s, with captives mostly male children and adolescents arriving by ship in this area. The captives were auctioned or sold directly from shipboard or dockside.

Over the years, especially during wars, Blacks were employed at the Portsmouth Naval Shipyard, established in 1800, the Navy's oldest continuously operating shipyard.

Though excluded from the Air Force, Marines, and Coast Guard, and accepted only in limited numbers by the Army and Navy, Black Americans comprised 16 percent of the World War II era armed forces while they comprised only 10 percent of the nation's population. They were banned from becoming officers and assigned to menial tasks. Late in the war they were finally allowed into combat and 4,500 Blacks served in segregated combat units in Europe. Among Black Portsmouth citizens in the armed services during World War II were Owen Finnigan Cooper (site 8), Eugene Reid, John Ramsay, Emerson Reed, Doris Moore, and Anna Jones.

---

* The original structure no longer exists
† No descriptive plaque

History cannot be unlived, but if faced with courage, can be freed from its shackles.

Among the first captives to these shores

Cuffee and Prince, sons of village royalty, play hunting games under the hot West African sun. Engrossed in their fantasy, the pair are unaware of slave traders stalking them. In a flash these children become commodities, an investment insured against loss, and are whisked away onto the sloop *Carolina,* making sail for the Americas.

Chained to each other and jammed below deck with other human cargo, the boys struggle to remain brave. Stormy seas toss the Carolina about and thunder shakes the ship to its core. Unlike many others, Cuffee and Prince survive the journey and spend most of the rest of their lives enslaved in the homes of William and Joseph Whipple of Portsmouth. (sites 14, 15, 18 & 26)

Cuffee and Prince mature into leadership roles in Portsmouth's growing Black community. In 1779 Prince is one of twenty men to sign an eloquent petition to end slavery in New Hampshire.

1779 Portsmouth petition sought end to slavery

Encouraged by the language of the Declaration of Independence, twenty Portsmouth men, including Prince Whipple, petitioned the General Assembly seeking their freedom. Two-hundred and thirty-four years later, in 2013, the petition finally was approved by the New Hampshire General Court. Excerpts of the original document:

The petition of Nero Brewster, and others, natives of Africa, now forcibly detained in slavery . . . most humbly sheweth, That the God of Nature gave them life and freedom, upon terms of the most perfect equality with other men; that freedom is an inherent right of the human species, not to be surrendered, but by consent, for the sake of social life; that private or public tyranny and slavery, are alike detestable to minds conscious of the equal dignity of human nature . . .

Your humble slaves most devoutly pray, for the sake of insured liberty, for the sake of justice, humanity, and the rights of mankind; for the honor of religion, and by all that is dear, that your honors would graciously interpose in our behalf, and enact such laws and regulations as in your wisdom . . . [that] we may regain our liberty and be rank'd in the class of free agents, and that the name of SLAVE may no more be heard in a land gloriously contending for the sweets of freedom. . . .

Portsmouth. Nov. 12, 1779

Sherburne House, Campus of Strawbery Banke Museum

The White Sherburnes built their steep-roofed house in two phases, c. 1695 and c. 1702, when the neighborhood was new. Joseph Sherburne was a mariner, merchant, and farmer. He lived here with his family and two enslaved people who are listed in a 1744 estate inventory as "one Negro man £200, one ditto woman £50." The man probably worked for Sherburne at sea, on the dock, in his store, and on his outlying farmland. The woman probably worked for Sherburne's wife, cooking, cleaning, textile production, and gardening. White Yankees typically assigned Black workers to sleeping space in attics, cellars, and back ells. The Black Sherburnes probably slept in the attic of this house.

South Meeting House, 280 Marcy St.

This 1866 Victorian election hall was home to two major institutions that affected the lives of Portsmouth's Black citizens. Starting on New Year's Day, 1881, annual celebrations of the Emancipation Proclamation were held here. The first was attended by "most of the colored people of the city" and more than 100 invited White guests. The celebration was an annual tradition for eighty years.

This building was also home to New Hampshire's first Black church, People's Mission, which moved into the building in 1890, after a multi-denominational Bible study class outgrew the capacity of James F. Slaughter's living room. In 1892 it reorganized into People's Baptist Church (site 27) and was an auxiliary of the Middle Street Baptist Church for sixteen years.

In the 1700s, this was the site of South Church (site 24), where Ona Judge (sites 31 & 35), who escaped from the household of George and Martha Washington, married John Staines in 1797.

Racially separate churches in America allowed worship in the African-American tradition and provided not only centers for social and political activities, but relief from the segregated seating and other limitations imposed by White religious institutions.

NH Gazette, 337 Pleasant St., Howard & Washington Streets [private]

Primus was one of a group of skilled enslaved people who worked in colonial Portsmouth. He was in the household of Daniel Fowle, owner of *The New Hampshire Gazette*, founded in 1756 in a small wood house that stood on this site. The household also included two enslaved women and the printer's wife. Primus operated Fowle's printing press for 50 years, first in Boston, then Portsmouth. At his master's death, he was bequeathed to John Melcher, a former printing apprentice who lived on Market Street. Primus was permanently stooped and "grieved by roguish boys" who probably teased him for his posture, age, and color. In his 90s, he was well known in town. A memorial poem in the newspaper described him as "a hearty friend" with a "grateful mind though borne down with pain." He died in May of 1791.

(*The Gazette*, the first paper in the province of New Hampshire, was revived by a direct descendant of its founder in 1989 and is published twice a month.)

---

* The original structure no longer exists

Cooper's House and Beauty Shop, 171 Washington St. [private]

Rosary Broxay Cooper came to Portsmouth from Florida as a children's nurse for the Merrill family, owners of a hotel in Ogunquit, Maine. In 1938 she married Portsmouth native Owen Finnegan Cooper (site 4). While he served as a master sergeant in the 509th Quartermaster Division in Europe during World War II, Rosary operated a twenty-ton crane at the Portsmouth Naval Shipyard. After the war, they returned to a segregated world. Finnegan worked as a messenger at City Hall. Rosary became Portsmouth's first licensed Black hairdresser. She operated her shop and a boarding house for Black people here in their sixteen-room home. When retired and widowed, Rosary volunteered on behalf of the New Hampshire Soldiers Home and the VFW Orphan's Home until her death in 1997.

---

† No descriptive plaque

Stoodley's Tavern, 14 Hancock St., Strawbery Banke Museum

James Stoodley's tavern, built in 1761, and originally located on Daniel Street (moved to Strawbery Banke in the 1970s), was believed to be built by Hopestill Cheswell (sites 21 & 37). It provided a gathering place for Revolutionary patriots, including Paul Revere, who stopped there in 1774. It was also a site for colonial auctions of bulk goods and sometimes enslaved people. Stoodley owned two enslaved Blacks—Frank and Flora. He also owned an expensive pew in North Church plus additional seating for Frank and Flora in the upper gallery. Sometime after the Revolution, Flora appears to have attained her freedom. She married a former slave, Cyrus Bruce (site 2), who was employed by Governor John Langdon.

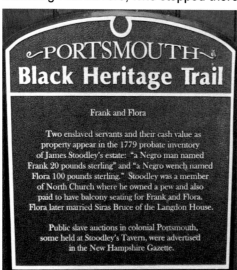

⌐PORTSMOUTH⌐
Black Heritage Trail

Frank and Flora

Two enslaved servants and their cash value as property appear in the 1779 probate inventory of James Stoodley's estate: "a Negro man named Frank 20 pounds sterling" and "a Negro wench named Flora 100 pounds sterling." Stoodley was a member of North Church where he owned a pew and also paid to have balcony seating for Frank and Flora. Flora later married Siras Bruce of the Langdon House.

Public slave auctions in colonial Portsmouth, some held at Stoodley's Tavern, were advertised in the New Hampshire Gazette.

Penhallow House, Washington Street, Strawbery Banke Museum

There were a few free Black people in colonial Portsmouth and increasing numbers were freed after the Revolution. To certify their status and exemption from slave curfew laws, free Black people secured freedom papers from their former owners. Some also registered with the town clerk or a justice of the peace such as Samuel Penhallow who lived in this house. In 1778, for example, when North Church (site 18) minister Ezra Stiles freed his enslaved man, Newport, they registered the manumission (formal freeing of an enslaved person) with the town clerk and with Justice Penhallow. Newport chose the surname Freeman.

Black people attained freedom in varied ways: through the will of a deceased owner; by living owners, sometimes in recognition of service in the Revolution; by buying their own freedom; and by running away. Status at birth followed status of the mother. Leisha Webb, a free Black woman, married Ceasor, an enslaved man, and eventually recorded with the town that she and her eight children were free persons.

Post-Revolutionary manumissions created the first significant free Black populations in America. Free Black Yankees in Portsmouth made homes where White convention allowed: as live-in paid help in White households, as boarders in minor waterfront lanes, in their own households at the outer edges of the compact part of town, or in scattered rural clusters. The Penhallow house was divided into apartments in the twentieth century and Black citizens of Portsmouth lived there.

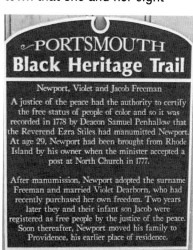

PORTSMOUTH
Black Heritage Trail

Newport, Violet and Jacob Freeman

A justice of the peace had the authority to certify the free status of people of color and so it was recorded in 1778 by Deacon Samuel Penhallow that the Reverend Ezra Stiles had manumitted Newport. At age 29, Newport had been brought from Rhode Island by his owner when the minister accepted a post at North Church in 1777.

After manumission, Newport adopted the surname Freeman and married Violet Dearborn, who had recently purchased her own freedom. Two years later they and their infant son Jacob were registered as free people by the justice of the peace. Soon thereafter, Newport moved his family to Providence, his earlier place of residence.

Warner House, 150 Daniel St.

The White colonial occupants of this 1716 brick house included its first owner, Archibald Macpheadris; Royal Governor Benning Wentworth, and merchant Jonathan Warner. But it was also home to at least eight enslaved people, including four enslaved by Macpheadris—a girl and three men (Prince, Nero, and Quamino).

Jonathan Warner's slaves were said to have lived in a small wood ell at the back of the brick house. Two, Cato and Peter, were among twenty African men who signed a petition to the legislature in 1779 to abolish slavery (site 14 and page 9). A third, John Jack, married Phillis, a formerly enslaved woman. She purchased land in Greenland, New Hampshire, in 1792. A few years later, Ona Judge Staines (site 35), a fugitive who escaped enslavement in the Philadelphia household of George and Martha Washington, was sheltered by them, along with her children.

† No descriptive plaque

Saint John's Church, 100 Chapel St.

Church records identify many Black people in early Portsmouth. An example is an 1807 entry in the Saint John's records: "Contribution Xmas day, Venus, a Black," a Christmas gift from the church to Venus. Her name, neither African nor Christian, is characteristic of names often given by Whites to separate the enslaved from their African heritage and from White society. The charitable gift indicates Venus was no longer in bondage; she was now free and poor. Her lack of a last name suggests she was single. Her association with Saint John's strongly suggests her former owner was a church member.

More than 150 years later, in 1963, local people gathered here to discuss race and religion. Seacoast Council on Race and Religion (SCORR) grew quickly, attracting Black and White citizens. SCORR members were at the Martin Luther King, Jr. March in Boston in April 1965 and raised funds for his work. They created a local speakers bureau, attended conferences on racism, and raised money for voter registration drives in Mississippi. They also met with seacoast chapters of the League of Women Voters, canvassed the local community on the status of civil rights, sponsored youth education programs, condemned local minstrel shows, and supported the 1968 Poor People's March on Washington. The organization disbanded in 1972.

Waterfront, Ceres Street

Enslaved mariners were part of the Portsmouth scene by 1727. They worked mostly in the Atlantic coastal and West Indies trades, and some sailed in the Revolution. In freedom, Black Yankees continued working at this dangerous and undesirable work in numbers disproportionate to their portion of the total population.

Most Black people in Portsmouth lived within a few blocks of the river. Jobs as mariners, stevedores, and truckmen were available in places like Ceres Street. At sea, the need to cooperate for safety in severe conditions and for mutual support against harsh captains fostered egalitarianism and friendships. Employers gave equal pay and rank to qualified Black mariners and some became officers on New England's whaling ships, partially because of the terrible danger involved. For instance, in February of 1845, William Wentworth, a local twenty-one-year-old Black mariner on a Portsmouth-based whaling ship, fell overboard and drowned in the Indian Ocean.

The reasonable pay of maritime work enabled some Black mariners to purchase modest homes, raise families, start businesses, or move to towns with more opportunities. However, mid-century brought change. Responsibility for hiring crews shifted from ship owners or captains to shipping masters, who hired White mariners over Black. By 1850, Black men at sea were limited to the roles of cook, steward, or cabin servant. By the 1860s Black mariners were remembered as a feature of Portsmouth's past.

Moffatt-Ladd House, 154 Market St.

The Moffatt-Ladd mansion is remembered as the home of Declaration of Independence signer, Brigadier General William Whipple. It was also the home of the Whipples' enslaved people, including Prince (site 15 and page 8) who accompanied his owner in Revolutionary War campaigns in Saratoga in 1777 and Rhode Island in 1778. Despite laws prohibiting Black militiamen, Prince was among many Black men who served.

Later he joined nineteen other Africa-born men in a bid for their own independence (page 9), submitting a petition on November 12, 1779 to the New Hampshire State Legislature. They described how they had been taken from Africa as children and invoked rationalist philosophy and Christian theology. In 1772, slavery was declared illegal in Britain and, implicitly, in the colonies. Even so, the New Hampshire Legislature, although it initially agreed to hear the petition, tabled it instead. Prince was granted his freedom February 26, 1784, although slavery was not formally abolished in New Hampshire until 1858.

A few people remained enslaved in New Hampshire as late as 1840.

Black Whipple House, 127 High St. [private]

In the mid 1700s, two African boys, Prince and Cuffee, reputedly from a wealthy family in Anomabou, Ghana, were sold to William and Joseph Whipple. Prince lived in the Moffatt-Ladd House (site 14) and Cuffee in the Joseph Whipple household (site 31).

Both were freed in 1784. When William Whipple died in 1785, his widow, respecting her husband's wishes, let Prince and Cuffee move a small house onto a lot in the back corner of the Moffat-Ladd House garden. Prince and Cuffee's families lived there together.

Prince worked as the chief steward at assemblies, balls, and weddings. Cuffee played fiddle at many of these events. Prince's wife, Dinah Chase, did cash work for North Church and conducted, in her home, a school for Black children, sponsored by the Ladies Charitable African Society. Both Prince and Dinah subscribed to the North Church Library. Prince died in 1796, after only twelve years of freedom. Cuffee died in 1816; his wife, Rebecca, in 1829.

In 1832, the house was considered a fire hazard and Dinah was moved, by the Whipple descendants, to a property on Pleasant Street. She died in 1846 in near poverty.

The Black Whipple Family

Prince and Cuffee Whipple, possibly brothers or cousins, had been owned by the white Whipples. The men were given lifelong use of this plot of land after their emancipation in the 1780s.. They moved a small wooden house onto the site and lived there with their wives, Dinah (Chase) and Rebecca (Daverson), and their children.

At assemblies and society balls Prince worked as a steward, Cuffee as a musician. Dinah did sewing for the North Church and with Rebecca kept a school in their home for Black children sponsored by the Ladies Charitable African Society.

* The original structure no longer exists

Meeting Rooms, 14-16 Market Square, Corner of Pleasant and Daniel Streets

In 1919, Our Boys' Comfort Club (soon renamed the Lincoln American Community Club) met on the upper floors of this building, offering social evenings for "colored enlisted men, Phillipinoe [*sic*], Porto Ricans [*sic*] and other darker racial groups in the service stationed in the area, as well as Civilian Colored people."

A Black lodge of the fraternal Knights of Pythias also met here around the same time. Other Black social groups in Portsmouth included the Colored Citizens League, which promoted unified action for civil rights; and the Octagon Club, Portsmouth's Black Masonic organization, affiliated with the Prince Hall Masonic Lodge in Boston. Such organizations provided vital mutual support during the resurgence of the Ku Klux Klan, active locally in the 1920s, and *de facto* segregation which endured in Portsmouth into the 1960s.

Town Pump & Stocks, beside North Church, Market Square

In Colonial New Hampshire, people suspected of crimes were subject to public punishment. In Portsmouth, a whipping post and stocks were near the town pump in Market Square, east of North Church, near Daniel Street. While public shaming and whipping were not limited to Blacks, enslaved people faced many laws that applied only to them.

In American slavery, Whites created a legal paradox in which the enslaved were sometimes treated as property, sometimes as people; usually oppressed and occasionally feared. In 1714, after hearing of a slave revolt in New York, the New Hampshire Assembly enacted a series of restrictions on concealing or transporting runaways. They also tried to forbid further importation of slaves and levied a tax on owners. Laws also exempted the colonial welfare system from supporting the children of any Black couples whose marriage was approved by their owners. (Owners assumed financial responsibility and ownership of the children of their enslaved women.)

Curfews were set periodically for "Indian, Negro, and Mulatto servants and slaves," with violation punishable by lashing, usually at the town pump that stood here in the town square on the east side of the North Meeting house (North Church, site 18). Conversely, in 1718 the New Hampshire Assembly forbade cruelty and maiming of servants and slaves and made killing them a capital crime.

> "Our work centers around creating an environment for racial justice, equity and healing. We foster change by providing a counter narrative that celebrates the resilience, versatility, courage and achievements of African Americans in New Hampshire. By dispelling myths that have led to systemic racism, we work to change hearts and minds."
> —JerriAnne Boggis, executive director, Black Heritage Trail of New Hampshire

* The original structure no longer exists
† No descriptive plaque

North Church, Market Square

In the colonial era, some White people objected to the Christianization of enslaved Africans and didn't take their slaves to church. But other Whites catechized their slaves and took them to church. Many enslaved people later were baptized and some became church members. Members or not, Blacks, whether they were enslaved or free, were isolated in Negro pews in most churches. At the end of the eighteenth century, when many were manumitted (set free), the number of Black churchgoers in Portsmouth increased. Many early Blacks were associated with North Church, including Frank and Flora Stoodley, (sites 2 & 9). A North Church minister married Prince Whipple (site 15) to Dinah Chase Whipple and Peter Warner (site 11) to Dinah Pearn.

Pomp & Candace Spring House & Bakery, Church & Porter Streets

Where there now is a bank parking lot, once stood the home of Pomp and Candace Spring, both formerly enslaved. They moved here shortly after marrying in 1793 and soon acquired adjacent land to build a bakery. Pomp, who served as president of the African Society, dressed impeccably in high fashion, even when delivering sea biscuits to outgoing ships and bread to local customers. Along with their bakery, the Springs also may have rented spare rooms in their well-appointed home. The couple died within four months of each other in 1807 and their obituaries noted they were friend to all in the city, both White and Black.

Caesar Whidden (site 30), also successful in business as a freedman, was Pomp Spring's brother-in-law and served as executor of his estate. Whidden arranged for the care of Pomp's mother, Phillis, their home and other assets, and commissioned matching gravestones for Pomp's and Candace's burials in Old North Cemetery (site 26).

Pomp and Candace Spring's matching gravestones, Old North Cemetery (site 26).

* The original structure no longer exists
† No descriptive plaque

 **Site 20 ***

Music Hall (The Temple), Chestnut & Congress Streets

Black abolitionists drove the changes that culminated in the Thirteenth Amendment to the Constitution in 1865. In Portsmouth, Black abolitionists spoke at the Temple, a 1,000-seat public lecture hall which opened in 1844. (An 1878 fire led to construction of the Music Hall on this site.)

Those abolitionists included Charles Lenox Remond. In his 1854 speech, he promoted practical approaches, including racially integrated abolition societies; employment of Blacks in non-menial jobs; integration of public transportation; Black voting rights in free states; and the need for Black businessmen to advocate abolition.

Another abolitionist, William Wells Brown, spoke October 12, 1862, three months before Lincoln signed the Emancipation Proclamation. He had escaped enslavement in Kentucky and lived in Buffalo and Boston. An accomplished author and international orator, he was among the first wave of abolitionists to define slavery as a sin that endangered the nation.

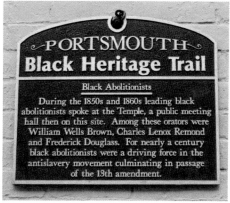

Frederick Douglass addressed the Portsmouth Female Anti-Slavery Society in December, 1844 at the Temple, returning as a famous orator March 15, 1862, to discuss *The Black Man's Future in the Southern States*. Douglass escaped from enslavement in 1838 in Maryland and settled in New Bedford, Massachusetts. He emphasized that so long as slavery existed in America, he was not a fugitive from slavery, but still a fugitive slave.

---

* The original structure no longer exists

John Paul Jones House, 43 Middle St.

This house is most famous for a short-term boarder—Revolutionary War Naval hero John Paul Jones, who spent a total of eighteen months in Portsmouth outfitting two war ships, the *Ranger* and the *America*. But, perhaps more interesting, is the man who built the house in 1758—Hopestill Cheswell (sites 9 & 36), a free African-American master housewright.

Cheswell's father, formerly enslaved, may have been the first Black man to own land in New Hampshire (deeded to him in 1717). Cheswell, like his father, married a White woman, Katherine Keniston. He earned enough with his building skills to buy several properties, including 100 acres of farmland, and to send his son, Wentworth (site 37), to the Governor Dummer Academy in Byfield, Massachusetts.

Another house built by Cheswell—the home of the Reverend Samuel Langdon, across the street from the Governor Langdon house (site 2)—eventually was moved to Old Sturbridge Village in Massachusetts.

† No descriptive plaque

Rockingham Hotel (Rockingham House), 401 State St. [private]

In 1948, New Hampshire resident Louis DeRochemont, famous for his *March of Time* newsreels, made *Lost Boundaries*, a controversial film loosely based on the biography of Black physician Albert C. Johnston of Keene, New Hampshire. DeRochemont did most of the filming in the seacoast and arranged to have his headquarters at the Rockingham Hotel. Proprietor James Barker Smith balked at having Black people on the premises. But under threat of losing DeRochemont's business, Smith changed his policy.

Many years later, July 4, 1964, Smith's other hotel, the Wentworth-by-The-Sea in nearby Newcastle, was the focus of a local NAACP desegregation action when three couples, two White and one Black, insisted on eating dinner there. Smith protested for several hours, even suggesting the Black couple could eat in the kitchen, but eventually conceded. Ironically, around the same time, the local NAACP branch moved its meetings to the Rockingham.

African Burying Ground Memorial Park, Chestnut Street, between State & Court Streets

AFRICAN BURYING GROUND MEMORIAL

In 1705, the Portsmouth government recorded the presence of a separate "Negro Burying Ground," likely called the African Burying Ground by the town's Black population at the outskirts of the riverfront town. Deaths among Portsmouth Blacks were from unhealthy living conditions, malnutrition, and hazardous work. Smallpox deaths are absent from the record, probably because many Black Americans practiced inoculation, a Muslim medical procedure slaves brought with them from sub-Sahara West Africa.

By 1760, Portsmouth's core had expanded to the area occupied by this burial ground and it may have been out of use by 1790. By 1813 the site was built over.

In October, 2003 city workers found thirteen coffins under a small area of Chestnut Street. Archaeologists removed eight to study and later reinter. As many as two hundred people may be buried there. The Portsmouth City Council appointed an African Burying Ground Committee to create a public place of honor and remembrance. The African Burying Ground Memorial Park, We Stand in Honor of Those Forgotten—is the result, designed with the help of sculptor Jerome Meadows.

We Stand in Honor of Those Forgotten

The "discovery" of the burying ground occurred at least twice before when work was done on the street. Both times it was barely mentioned and sewer lines were laid directly through some of the coffins.

But in 2003 the site was not ignored. Planning and celebration of the renewed sacred space engaged many in the city for a dozen years, including city and state officials, dancers, poets, artists, musicians, clergy, historians, archeologists, and schoolchildren. Ceremonies and celebrations included a dance and poetry

Chestnut Street, photo is marked where several graves were believed to be located under the street.

project, a consecration ceremony when work began on the park, and an all-night vigil at New Hope Baptist Church (site 33) where the remains of eight exhumed enslaved people awaited reinternment the next morning, May 23, 2015.

Memorial designer and artist, Jerome Meadows of Savannah, Georgia, wrote a poem that is etched on the silhouette figures at one end of the park:

> *I stand for the Ancestors Here and Beyond*
> *I stand for those who feel anger*
> *I stand for those who were treated unjustly*
> *I stand for those who were taken from their loved ones*
> *I stand for those who suffered the middle passage*
> *I stand for those who survived upon these shores*
> *I stand for those who pay homage to this ground*
> *I stand for those who find dignity in these bones.*

The remains of thirteen African or African descent persons, removed from the burying ground for study, are returned and reinterred in plain pine coffins the day the park is dedicated during Memorial Day weekend in 2015.

Artist Jerome Meadows said he debated a long time whether or not the hands of the man and woman in his sculpture should be touching. The Portsmouth committee overseeing the work decided they should be almost touching.

Aerial photo: David J. Murray, ClearEyePhoto.com

South Church, 292 State St.

The earliest identifiable Black family in Portsmouth appears in the South Church records of baptism in 1717. More than 150 years later, South Church's Unitarian women are reputed to have participated in the Underground Railroad, helping fugitive slaves leave the country. After the Civil War, they founded, funded, and operated schools for newly-freed Black Americans. As many as one hundred students, ranging from infants to elderly, were instructed together. In the twentieth century, South Church members were active in the local civil rights movement, and their ministers were guest preachers at Portsmouth's People's Baptist Church (site 27).

The Unitarian-Universalist South Church (pictured here) was built in 1824. The congregation originally met in the South Parish, replaced in 1866 by the South Meeting House (site 6).

Education is the most powerful tool to craft a better future.

"Discovering New Hampshire's hidden Black history has changed our whole perspective of the state, and our sense of how we belong."

—BHTNH interns Shetarrah and Jubilee Byfield

Beyond Downtown Portsmouth

Beyond downtown are locations that help tell the story of Portsmouth's Black community, especially as the city grew north and west. Many of these sites are still being researched, so there are few plaques; other Black-owned businesses and residences in this area were lost to urban renewal in the 1960s.

The trail is walkable for the energetic. Jackson Hill (site 25) is about a mile from the end of the Downtown Trail and it's another mile to Union Street (sites 29 & 30).

The full Beyond Downtown trail is about three miles.

Beyond Downtown Portsmouth Map Key

25 *Jackson Hill, Jackson & Northwest Streets, off Maplewood Avenue

26 Old North Cemetery, Maplewood Avenue

27 The Pearl (People's Baptist Church), 45 Pearl St.

28 †Elizabeth Virgil House, 50 Brewster St. [private]

29 †Haywood Burton House, 179 Union St. [private]

30 *†John Francis House, Union Street

31 †Joseph Whipple House, 599 Middle St., across from Cass St. [private]

SITE KEY

* The original structure no longer exists

† No descriptive plaque

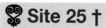
Jackson Hill, Jackson Hill & Northwest Streets, off Maplewood Avenue

This area has been home to African-Americans for centuries. It is also the site of New Hampshire's oldest remaining wood house, the Richard Jackson House, built in 1664. The earliest Black residents, including Prince Jackson, were enslaved by local families. In the nineteenth century, Isabelle Grimm, who was born in Virginia, lived in several locations on Jackson Hill Street. Isabelle, known as Belle, became the wife of Jacob Tilley in 1886. A washerwoman by trade, she gave birth to at least six children and also took in boarders. When Mary Jackson Brown inherited the historic Jackson house in 1897, Belle Tilley was a tenant there. Belle and her son Clarence retained life residency rights to the Jackson house, staying until 1947, although the house, after more than 250 years of ownership by the Jackson heirs, was sold in 1924 to the founder of the Society for the Preservation of New England Antiquities.

† No descriptive plaque

Old North Cemetery, Maplewood Avenue

Valerie Cunningham at Prince Whipple's burial site (the white gravestone pictured to the left of flag), Old North Cemetery, Maplewood Ave.

Markers identify burial sites of Prince Whipple (sites 14 & 15; see also pages 8 and 9); his daughter, Esther Whipple Mullinaux; her daughter, Elizabeth Smith; and Pomp and Candace Spring (site 19). Dinah, Prince's wife, is believed to be buried near her husband. The cemetery dates back to 1753.

People's Baptist Church (The Pearl), 45 Pearl St.

Pearl Street Church, circa 1897-1901. Courtesy of Portsmouth Athenaeum.

In 1908, People's Baptist Church separated from Middle Street Baptist Church. It met for worship in the South Meeting House (site 6) on Marcy Street, near the waterfront. But as the center of activity shifted from the waterfront toward the North Mill Pond area and the city's Plains (site 32), it was appropriate for the church also to move. In 1915, under the leadership of Reverend John L. Davis, it purchased this former Free Will Baptist Church. For fifty years, People's Baptist Church welcomed pulpit exchanges with neighboring churches and Baha'is. Guest preachers included Reverend Martin Luther King, Jr., in 1952 when he was a doctoral student at Boston University. People's Baptist Church was succeeded by New Hope Baptist Church in 1964, moving to Peverly Hill Road in 1969 (site 33).

Elizabeth Virgil House, 50 Brewster St. [private]

Elizabeth Virgil, in 1926, was the first African-American to graduate with a bachelor's degree from the University of New Hampshire. She grew up in the Puddle Dock area of Portsmouth, the daughter of a chef and a housekeeper, and the granddaughter of an emancipated slave. Elizabeth always wanted to be a teacher, but, even with UNH teaching credentials, she could not be hired to teach in the predominately white classrooms of New England. So she taught school for several years in the segregated South. She returned to Portsmouth in the 1940s to tend to her ailing mother and a disabled sister, but was still closed out of teaching positions because of her race. Instead, she made a living as a clerk typist first at the Shipyard

Elizabeth Ann Virgil (right) with her sister, Melvina Parker, circa 1925–1930s. Courtesy of Portsmouth Athenaeum.

and then, for twenty-two years, at UNH, where she typed field notes for soil conservationists. She purchased this house in 1955. After retiring, Elizabeth sang in three community choirs, traveled around the world, and volunteered with the Red Cross. She died at age eighty-seven, just three months after the university commissioned her portrait, which now hangs in the university's Dimond Library.

---

† No descriptive plaque

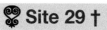

Haywood Burton home, 179 Union St. [private]

Haywood Burton, known as the Black mayor of Portsmouth in the 1930s, '40s, and '50s, was a founder of People's Baptist Church (site 27), where he held multiple roles, including deacon, Sunday school superintendent, and trustee. Born in Virginia, he came to Portsmouth as a young man, working first as a footman for a physician, later promoted to coachman. He was a janitor at Portsmouth Hospital for eighteen years. He also ran a café and catering business, and was a landlord, notary public, and justice of the peace.

† No descriptive plaque

John Francis House, Union Street

In the early 1800s, Caesar Whidden (site 19), an emancipated Black man, acquired and sold several residential properties (c. 211-235 Union Street) to other Blacks, including John Francis who bought a house lot for $200 in 1808. Soon after the War of 1812, prominent Portsmouth merchants John and Nathaniel Haven built Francis a house on or next to that lot in gratitude for service rendered by him during the War. Francis was working aboard one of the Havens' ships when it was captured by privateers. He hid the proceeds of selling the ship's cargo, 15,000 dollars in coins, in the bottom of a slush tub (used to hold grease waste from the ship's kitchen). When the boat landed, Francis begged for the old slush tub as his payment. He got the tub and its sixty pounds of gold, which he returned to the Haven brothers.

Historical accounts differ on whether John Francis' house was two or four houses up on the east side of Union Street from Middle Street. This, however, might have been his house, described by Charles W. Brewster, in 1859 in Rambles About Portsmouth. *Decades later another historian noted the house closer to Middle, describing it as near a former stocking factory.*

---

* The original structure no longer exists
† No descriptive plaque

Joseph Whipple House, 599 Middle St. [private]

In the fall of 1796, Colonel Joseph Whipple (site 15), the collector of customs in Portsmouth, was asked to help return Ona Judge (site 35), to the household of President Washington. Whipple, a Washington appointee, reported that he met with Ona, possibly in his customs office, the extension on the right side of this house. He wrote that Ona was willing to return to the Washington home if promised her freedom when they died. That promise was not forthcoming and Whipple reported his efforts had failed. Ona spent the rest of her life as a fugitive living in the Seacoast and raising a family. This house initially was on State Street, across from the African Burying Ground (site 23).

---

† No descriptive plaque

Related Sites

Black experience in the seacoast extended to the edges of Portsmouth where an annual colonial Black celebration was held (site 32) and farther to where the White Langdon family buried some of its enslaved people. Sites 35, 36, and 37 are in other towns. **These sites are best reached by car.**

Map Key to Related Portsmouth Sites

32 The Plains, Middle Road (Route 33) at Islington Street, Portsmouth

33 New Hope Baptist Church, 263 Peverly Road, Portsmouth

34 Langdons' Slave Cemetery, 1035 Lafayette Rd., (Route 1), adjacent to Christ Episcopal Church Rectory, Portsmouth

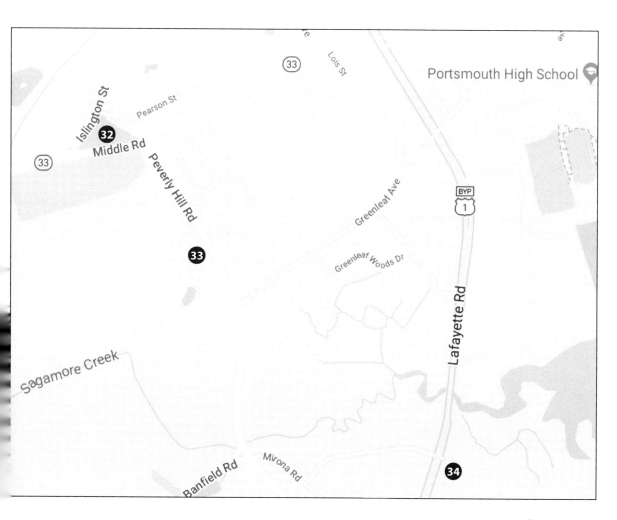

The Plains, Middle Road (Route 33) at Islington Street, Portsmouth

In colonial Portsmouth, as throughout the Americas, a coronation or election of Black leaders was held each June, conducted in West African style and based loosely on such celebrations as the spring Odwira festival of the Ashanti people of Ghana in which society was purified, leaders were recognized, community was sanctified, and ancestors were honored. Black people assembled in bright clothing and, accompanied by lively music and boisterous gunfire, marched to a broad open space. In Portsmouth they gathered here at the Plains. Nero Brewster was elected king repeatedly. Jock Odiorne was sheriff and Willie Clarkson was viceroy.

After the elections, there was food, drink, music, dance, and games. The festivities presumably occurred at the Bell Tavern on Congress Street, owned by Brewster's master. This event helped forge Africans from disparate tribes into a single Afro-American community and contributed to the transmission of African cultural values to a new generation. King Nero died in 1786. Coronations in New England disappeared in the early 1800s as the Africa-born generation passed away.

New Hope Baptist Church, 263 Peverly Hill Rd., Portsmouth

Because American evangelical worship paralleled West African spiritual tradition in some ways, Portsmouth's nineteenth century Black Christians were drawn toward evangelical churches. Portsmouth had two White Baptist churches in the colonial period. Later, Portsmouth's first Black church was also Baptist. Several former members of People's Baptist Church (site 27) were among the founders of New Hope Baptist Church. New Hope continues to flourish, providing an important spiritual resource and social center to many in the Seacoast's community. Its pastor and congregants were among the founders of the Portsmouth Black Heritage Trail.

Langdons' Slave Cemetery, 1035 Lafayette Rd., (Route 1), adjacent to Christ Episcopal Church Rectory, Portsmouth

Jubilee Byfield and visiting public historian Elon Cook Lee, at the Langdon Slave Burial Ground

Rural families often established family burial grounds on their property rather than using centrally-located town burial grounds. When such households included enslaved Black people, segregation was customary. According to oral tradition, this burial ground on one of the Langdon family's farms was their slave burial ground, including those who moved seasonally from the Langdons' in-town residence (site 2) to the outlying farms as their labor was needed. The uninscribed boulders used as markers contrast with the engraved marble monuments in a nearby burial ground for the White Langdons.

🪬 Site 35 * †

Ona Maria Judge Staines Home, Greenland, NH [private]

(This site is still being researched. For more information, visit Weeks Library, 35 Post Road, Greenland)

Twenty-two-year-old Ona Maria Judge (sites 2, 6, 11 & 31), enslaved by President and Martha Washington, escaped from the executive mansion in Philadelphia in 1796 and boarded the sloop *Nancy*, headed for Portsmouth, New Hampshire.

The free Black communities in Philadelphia and Portsmouth aided Ona, helping her escape, hide, and find work sewing and housekeeping in Portsmouth.

In 1797 she married Black seafarer Jack Staines in Portsmouth. Staines died at sea in 1803 and Ona and her children moved in with the formerly enslaved John Jack (site 11) and his wife, Phillis, of Greenland. Phillis died in 1804, but Ona resided with Phillis' daughters until she died at age 74 in 1848, having outlived all her own children.

"*I am free now*"

This drawing of Ona Judge hangs on the wall of the memorial site of the Presidents' house in Philadelphia. George Washington offered a $10 reward for the return of "Oney Judge," described in the ad he ran in The Pennsylvania Gazette *as: "... a light mulatto girl, much freckled, with very black eyes and bushy hair. She is of middle stature, slender, and delicately formed, about 20 years of age. She has many changes of good clothes, of all sorts ..."*

---

* The original structure no longer exists
† No descriptive plaque

Rock Rest, 167 Brave Boat Harbor Rd., Kittery Point, Maine [private]

African-Americans vacationing in the Piscataqua Region. Undated photograph. Courtesy of Valerie Cunningham.

Hazel and Clayton Sinclair met while in domestic service in York, Maine, and lived in Portsmouth as newlyweds. In 1938 they purchased a home in Maine and used it as a summer guest house that welcomed African-Americans from 1947 to 1972, during the age of *de facto segregation* in the North. Rock Rest did not need to promote its business in the *Green Book* as some regional Black owned businesses did, word of mouth kept the inn full. The couple was active in the community on both sides of the Piscataqua River, including the Portsmouth NAACP and churches. Hazel was a member of the York League of Women Voters; Clayton served on a Kittery town board; and they both worked at the Naval Shipyard. Their picturesque home, Rock Rest, was listed on the National Register of Historic Places in 2008, and the Smithsonian's National Museum of African-American History and Culture has items from that house as part of its permanent collection.

---

† No descriptive plaque

Cheswell Cemetery, South Main Street, Newmarket, New Hampshire

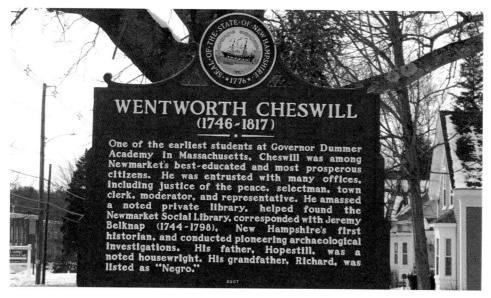

Wentworth Cheswell, son of colonial master house builder Hopestill Cheswell (sites 9 & 21), is noted as the first elected African-American public official in the United States. He held a range of public offices in Newmarket from 1768 until his death in 1817. Wentworth established the family cemetery.

---

† No descriptive BHTNH plaque

Our Programs

The Black Heritage Trail of New Hampshire, formed in 2017, has its roots in the Portsmouth Black Heritage Trail. Community partners have included the Portsmouth Library, the Portsmouth Antheneum, the University of New Hampshire, Strawbery Banke Museum, Seacoast African-American Cultural Center, Langdon House, Moffatt-Ladd House, Portsmouth Historical Society, the City of Portsmouth, and many community churches.

Sankofa Guided Walking Tours

More than 30 historic sites, many marked with plaques, tell the story of Blacks in Portsmouth, from the 1600s to now. Tour themes range from the New Hampshire slave trade to the civil rights movement. Guided tours are offered Saturdays May to October and by appointment. Visit blackheritagetrailnh.com for up to date information.

Sankofa Trolley Tours

Recently added, the trolley tours provide an hour-and-a-half guided tour of Portsmouth in an open-air trolley. These tours offer an overview of Portsmouth's Black heritage for those who prefer an alternative to walking. Trolley tours are offered May through September.

> "By sharing a truer history of the state, we are working toward eliminating stereotypes and we start thinking differently about who our neighbors are."
> —Rev. Robert Thompson, BHTNH board chair

Elinor Williams Hooker Tea Talks

The increasingly popular tea talks are held in the Portsmouth Public Library on Sundays, February to March. Speakers are engaging and topics are current and provocative. For more information visit blackheritagetrailnh.org/tea-talks/

Juneteenth Celebration

This is an annual, day-long celebration in Portsmouth commemorating the June 19, 1865 announcement of the abolition of slavery in Texas. The enslaved there finally gained their freedom on that day even though slavery had officially ended in 1863.

Black New England Conference

A two-day, annual conference, held in collaboration with the University of New Hampshire, gathers scholars, teachers, researchers, community members, and representatives of local organizations to share insights on the Black experience in northern New England. Conference themes have included science, literature, politics, humor, sports, and race.

Lenten Program

BHTNH collaborated with the Episcopal Church of New Hampshire to offer a collection of short readings on 40 little known historic figures from New Hampshire's African American community for the Episcopalians' 2018 Lenten Program. The stories and prayers are available to read on the website at: blackheritagetrailnh.org/2018-lenten-program/.

Spring Symposium

Topics in this annual, all-day workshop/symposium have included race and law, the underground railroad, and Blacks in film and TV. Visit blackheritagetrailnh.org/2018-spring-symposium/.

Reading Frederick Douglass

Each year on or near the Fourth of July, people gather to read out loud a speech delivered in 1852 by the eloquent abolitionist Frederick Douglass.

> *"This Fourth of July is yours, not mine.*
> *You may rejoice, I must mourn."*
>
> —Frederick Douglass, July 4, 1852

Milford Walking Tour

The director of BHTNH, JerriAnne Boggis, lives in Milford and has created a Black history trail there that focuses on Milford native and eighteenth-century author Harriet E. Wilson. The trail also highlights the abolitionist movement in the town.

Hancock Walking Tour

Tour Guide Eric Aldrich leads an interesting adventure through the hidden areas of Hancock, NH to explore cellar holes and share the forgotten stories of the town's Black settlers. Visit blackheritagetrailnh.com for up to date tour information.

Statewide Plans

BHTNH has plans to expand to the seven regions of the state starting in towns with solid documented Black history. Towns slated for immediate expansion are Exeter, Greenland, Newmarket, Canterbury, Keene, Jaffrey, Mason, Andover, Canaan, Newport, Warner, Pittsfield, and Hancock. Other towns will be added as more research is done. For expanded information on the BHTNH please visit blackheritagetrailnh.org

School Collaborations & Preservation Projects

Collaborations include working with high school students on a mural on the life of Elizabeth Virgil (site 28), and with the Moffatt-Ladd House and the high school on a study of the 1779 Portsmouth petition to end slavery (page 9).

Historic and Cultural Preservation

BHTNH initiated documentation and structural preservation of the Pearl Street Church (site #27) and the Rock Rest guesthouse (site #36). These and other related archival materials are deposited at UNH Dimond Library Special Collections

Artist-in-Residence

BHTNH partnered with Historic New England's Governor John Langdon House (site 2) and artist, Richard Haynes, during the summer of 2018 for an on-site residency that included youth workshops, a public forum, and open studio demonstrations while creating a portrait of Cyrus Bruce, the celebrated servant of the state's first governor.

For updates on BHTNH programs and events, visit:

blackheritagetrailnh.org

SHADOWS FALL NORTH

A Documentary

How does a state with the motto "Live Free or Die" and a celebrated legacy of abolitionism confront and understand its participation in slavery, segregation, and the neglect of African-American history?

Shadows Fall North seeks to answer the question: What happens when we move toward a fuller understanding of our history by including all voices?

This engaging documentary focuses on the efforts of two dedicated historic preservationists and activists, Valerie Cunningham (co-author of *Black Portsmouth: Three Centuries of African American Heritage*) of Portsmouth and JerriAnne Boggis of Milford, to recover the stories of people who have been rendered nearly invisible in the historical record, from individuals laid to rest at the **African Burying Ground in Portsmouth** to the **novelist Harriet Wilson** of Milford to the twenty slaves who petitioned the state legislature for their freedom in 1779… and many more.

For more information on the film, including details about screenings and DVD availability, please contact the University of New Hampshire Center for the Humanities, phone (603) 862-4356 or email humanities.center@unh.edu.

Read more about the project on the web at: **www.blackhistorynh.com**

54

Acknowledgments

This publication was made possible through a grant from the **Robins deBeaumont Foundation**. We would like to thank the Foundation for supporting this project and the work of the Black Heritage Trail of New Hampshire.

We are grateful to all our supporters including:

New Hampshire Charitable Foundation
The Springer Fund
The James R. Carter Fund
Dan & Blythe Brown Foundation
Sawtelle Family Fund
Geoffrey E. Clark & Martha Fuller Clark Fund
Ralph E. Ogdon Foundation
Winter Wheat Foundation
Endowment for Health
New Hampshire Humanities
Charles DeGrandpre, Esq.
Thomas Hooker
John Langdon Marsh
Frank & Irja Cilluffo
Tonya Singer
Sandra Ward
Barbara Sweet
Rita Weathersby
Yvonne Goldsberry
Skye & John Maher
Anne Howells Charitable Trust
Jackie Ellis
Alex Herlihy
Janet & Peter Prince
Irene & John Bush
David Watters
Angela Matthews
Robert & Nadine Thompson
Dennis Britton
JerriAnne Boggis
Peter Lamb
Nancy and Brian Vawter
Atlantic Media
Jeff and Martha Leathe
Great Life Press
Diocese of NH Episcopal Church

Exeter Hospital
Eversource
Northeast Delta Dental
Patrick Dorow Productions
Fabulous Find
Showing Up for Racial Justice
TD Bank
Eastern Bank Charitable Foundation
Kennebunk Savings Bank
Maine Community Foundation
Center for Humanities, UNH
The Center for New England Culture, UNH

Many Thanks to Our Volunteers!
Anne Arnold
Alys Barton
Kirsten Barton
Jubilee Byfield
Mary Jane Clark
Rose Correll
Catherine Greeley
Sally Hirshberg
Linda Keeffe
Angela Matthews
Terese Pawletko
Brad Randolph
Freddye Ross
Carolyn Saunders
Ken Schoman
Sara Schoman
Nur Shoop
Valerie Sousa
Diane Stradling
Nancy Vawter
Brian Vawter
Janis Wolak
Cathy Wolff

Valerie Cunningham

Imagine if you can, an eight-year-old child scouring all the books in her hometown library with the hopes of seeing a reflection of her community on those pages. This was the beginning of Valerie Cunningham's life long quest to celebrate and make visible New Hampshire's Black history.

It was during the turbulent '60s that she documented the early history of Africans in New Hampshire, laying a foundation for the Portsmouth Black Heritage Trail, which became a model for historic preservation nationwide.

JerriAnne Boggis

Imagine your five-year-old son running to you, distraught: "Mommy, what's a n-----? Molly wants to know how I could live with one." Growing up in Jamaica where she represented the majority, JerriAnne Boggis was oblivious to stereotypes conjured by skin. In Milford, she fed her biracial sons fables of the best-of-both-worlds, coffee-and-cream, that were instantly shattered by a pre-schooler. Other incidents would happen to highlight her *otherness*.

When she learned of the eighteenth-century African-American author Harriet E. Wilson, a native of Milford, that all changed. She was transformed. With a renewed sense of belonging, Boggis worked to have Wilson remembered and memorialized. She later joined with Valerie Cunningham on the Seacoast, which led to the creation of the Black Heritage Trail of New Hampshire.

Made in the USA
Columbia, SC
10 March 2021

33893514R00038